PERCY'S MEMOIR OF GOLDSMITH

THE HISTORY & SOURCES
OF PERCY'S
MEMOIR OF GOLDSMITH

By

KATHARINE C. BALDERSTON, Ph.D.
*Assistant Professor of English Literature
in Wellesley College*

CAMBRIDGE
AT THE UNIVERSITY PRESS
1926

CAMBRIDGE
UNIVERSITY PRESS

University Printing House, Cambridge CB2 8BS, United Kingdom

Cambridge University Press is part of the University of Cambridge.

It furthers the University's mission by disseminating knowledge in the pursuit of education, learning and research at the highest international levels of excellence.

www.cambridge.org
Information on this title: www.cambridge.org/9781107487383

© Cambridge University Press 1926

First published 1926
First paperback edition 2015

A catalogue record for this publication is available from the British Library

ISBN 978-1-107-48738-3 Paperback

PREFACE

The following study of Bishop Percy's biography of Goldsmith attempts only to trace its obscure genesis, and to point out the exact sources from which it was drawn. I hope, however, that my analysis may help to prepare the way for a new biography of the poet, by facilitating a revaluation of the contemporary sources of information. Of the need for a new biography, no student can doubt who has attempted to unravel the baffling web of fact and myth which his standard biographies present.

This study originally formed part of a dissertation presented to the faculty of Yale University for the degree of Doctor of Philosophy. My warmest thanks are due to Professor C. B. Tinker for directing me to the subject, and for his continuous and invaluable help. I gratefully acknowledge the generosity of Miss Constance Meade in permitting me to examine her unique collection, as well as the kindness of Mr W. M. Elkins, Mr Harold Murdock, and Mr R. B. Adam, in allowing me to use unpublished correspondence in their collections. Dr Paget Toynbee and Professor G. C. Moore Smith have likewise given me indispensable aid.

K. C. B.

SEPTEMBER 1925

THE HISTORY AND SOURCES OF
PERCY'S MEMOIR OF GOLDSMITH

BISHOP PERCY's Memoir of Goldsmith, prefixed to the edition of Goldsmith's *Works*, issued by the principal members of the London
book-trade in 1801, was the first considerable
authentic biography of the poet, and has remained
to this day the basis for a large part of the more
ambitious biographies which have superseded it. It
has proved a puzzle to all later investigators of Goldsmith's life, both because of the inexplicable delays
attending its preparation, and the involved question
of its authorship, and also because of the uncertainty
as to the exact character and provenance of the
original documents on which it was largely based.
Most of these original documents disappeared completely after the publication of the Memoir, and it
thus became the sole source of information concerning such important biographical evidence as
Mrs Hodson's narrative of her brother Oliver's early
life, Goldsmith's memorandum of his own life dictated to Percy in 1773, and the large number of
original letters it contained. These documents only
recently came to light again, in the possession of
Miss Constance Meade, a descendant of Bishop
Percy's, living in London, by whose courtesy the
present writer has been permitted to examine them.
These documents, and the discovery of a number of
hitherto unpublished, or only partially published,

letters of Percy, make it possible to trace consecutively for the first time the history of the Memoir's genesis and publication, and to determine the sources of Percy's information.

THE HISTORY OF THE MEMOIR

Short accounts of the Percy Memoir have been given by Prior[1] and Forster[2]. Prior's account, though invaluable because of the extracts it affords from Percy's and Malone's correspondence from MS. collections then in the possession of Dr H. U. Thomson and Mr William R. Mason, is too fragmentary to be satisfactory, and Forster's, beside being incomplete, errs in its too partisan effort to exonerate Bishop Percy from all the blame of the misunderstanding with the booksellers. Both leave in obscurity the time at which the office of biographer was transferred from Percy to Johnson, and back again to Percy; the reasons for the delay which permitted twenty-eight years to elapse before the publication of the Memoir, by which time all Goldsmith's relatives who were originally intended to benefit by the edition were dead; the reason for the change from Campbell to Boyd as ostensible editor; and the share of the three collaborators and of Rose, the "interpolator," in the final Memoir. These points will be duly considered here. No attempt, however, will be made to include the complications of Percy's con-

---

[1] *Life of Goldsmith*, London, 1837, I, pp. x–xiv.
[2] *Life and Times of Oliver Goldsmith*, 5th ed., London, 1871, II, 442–451.

nection with Goldsmith's surviving relatives, except when necessary to elucidate the progress of the Memoir. It will suffice to remind the reader that the original purpose of the friends of Goldsmith, in planning the edition, was to benefit Maurice Goldsmith, his younger brother, with whom they became acquainted on his visit to London to settle his brother's affairs, after Goldsmith's death. Charles, his other surviving brother, was out of touch with his family, and Catherine Hodson, his sister, was not in need. Presumably his other sister, Jane Johnson, who was indigent, did not survive him. Maurice died in the winter of 1792–3, and Henry Goldsmith's daughter, Catherine, and Maurice's widow, Esther, then presented themselves as rival claimants on the *Works in futuro*. Percy settled the claim in favour of Catherine, on her own information that Esther had remarried, and that her husband had left her handsomely provided for. She lived only until July, 1803, when as yet no settlement had been made by the Dublin bookseller entrusted with the sale of the copies designed for her benefit[1]. From an unpublished letter in the possession of Mr W. M. Elkins of Philadelphia, written by Percy to Malone on October 5, 1803, it appears that not until after Catherine's death did Percy divert any of the funds to the assistance of Charles, the youngest brother, who had returned to England from Jamaica in 1791, and who in 1795 had applied to Percy for a share in his

[1] The facts about Percy's negotiations with Catherine and Charles Goldsmith are taken from Clarke, *Trans. Bib. Soc.* XV, 51–58.

Goldsmith charity. Percy had at first paid no heed to his request because, upon inquiring of Catherine, he had been informed that her uncle had a "great deal of money in the funds." The pertinent passage of the letter to Malone, referred to above, reads:

I have a further favour to request of you. I had above a year ago[1] a letter from Charles Goldsmith, a Brother of the Poet, dated from No. 1 Dorset Place, St. Pancras, informing me that having formerly lived in Jamaica, he was come to reside in London, where he had purchased some property and that he had a little son named Oliver to whom he meant to give a liberal education and requesting for him some of the profit arising from the sale of his brother's works. At that time I had devoted this for the benefit of the author's niece in great indigence. But she is now dead, and I should be glad to give what copies remain unsold in London to this Mr. Chas. Goldsmith. But I have no answer to a letter I wrote to him on the subject (directed to him at about several months past.) And I requested a friend to inquire for him, who I believe had left town. Will you have the goodness to let your servant inquire if this Charles Goldsmith be dead or removed from the foregoing residence where I understood he lived in a house of his own, having built several houses there with some fortune he realized in Jamaica.

Charles, it is known, was finally located by Malone's friend, Bindley, who discovered that he had spent the time since the Peace of Amiens in France, and had returned to England to escape Napoleon's edict against British subjects.[2] For Charles' subsequent benefit from the *Works*, and his death on or near March 24, 1805, the reader is referred to Clarke's

---

[1] This refers to a second begging letter from Charles.
[2] Nichols, *Illust*. VIII, 239.

account,[1] and to Forster. Of other details of Percy's aid to the Goldsmith family Clarke gives the best account.

To return to the history of the Memoir itself. There can be no doubt that in Goldsmith's lifetime both he and Percy intended that the latter should be his biographer. The idea originated probably with Percy rather than with Goldsmith, for, as far as we know, Goldsmith, in spite of his life-long hunger for fame, had singularly little concern for biographical immortality. He wrote few letters, he made no effort to preserve records of his intimacy with the greatest men of his day, he left with his best friends only the haziest ideas of his youth, and of his early life in London before he gained prominence. None of them knew his birth-day or birth-place, or even his age, when he died. I surmise, then, that Percy was responsible for the suggestion which led Goldsmith, on April 28, 1773, in the flush of the success of *She Stoops to Conquer*, to visit Percy at Northumberland House, and there dictate to him a memorandum of his own life. This MS., still surviving in the Meade collection, is in Bishop Percy's own hand, and is endorsed by him with the exact date. It consists of six folio sheets of writing paper, folded, and roughly stitched by hand into a quarto pamphlet of twenty-four pages. Only twelve pages are used for the original memorandum, the remainder consisting of additional sheets on which Percy has written corrections. The first page of these is labelled, "Corrections from Dr. Goldsmith's Brother Maurice,"

[1] "Family Letters of Oliver Goldsmith," *Trans. Bib. Soc.* xv, 11–58.

and presumably this describes the later corrections as well. Sometimes, when no blank sheet offered, corrections were made between the lines of the text itself. All statements which seemed questionable to Percy were underlined, including a number for which no actual correction was offered. The text of this singular document, only part of which has been previously published,[1] is here reproduced, in order that Percy's use of it, and his deviations from it, in the published Memoir, may be clearly seen. The original state of the text is adhered to, including Percy's underlinings[2], and the corrections are given in the foot-notes. The family tree which comes first, on the cover of the pamphlet, is not a part of the original memorandum, but is on one of the correction sheets, and was evidently worked out by Percy at his leisure, from information given in the memorandum.

MEMOIRS OF DR. OLIVER GOLDSMITH

(Chiefly from his own Mouth, 1773.)   April 28.

Juan Romero = - - - - - - Goldsmith

John Goldsmith = O. Crafton
Gent.

| Jane Goldsmith, mard. Revd. Thos. Contarini | Charles Goldsmith = Ann, d. of Revd. Rector of Kilkenny *Theophl*.[3] Jones West |

1. Katharine   2. Henry   3. Jane   4. Dr Oliver Goldsmith the Poet   5. Maurice   6. Charles   7. John

[1] Clarke, *Nineteenth Cent.* LXXV, 821–831.
[2] Printed in italics.   [3] "Oliver" is added.

From his own Mouth, Apr. 28, 1773.

Dr. Oliver Goldsmith is Descended from a Spanish Family of the name of Romeiro or Romero, wch. came over to England[1] *in the time of Philip and Mary.*[2] From a marriage with a Miss Goldsmith the Descendents took the latter name.

His, the Doctor's, Father, the Revd. Charles Goldsmith, was a native of the *County of Durham,*[3] but educated at Dublin College: he got a small Living in England, & afterwds. a good Benefice in Ireland: being rector of Kilkenny West. He died while his son Oliver was at College (about 25 years ago, 1773). *General Wolfe was allied to the Goldsmith Family.*

His mother was Ann, Daughter of the Revd. Mr. Jones, Rector of Elphin. Her maternal Uncle & Grandfather & other of her Family has been successively Rectors of Kilkenny West aforesd. *She was allied to Oliver Cromwell, in compliment to whom our Author was named Oliver.*

They had 7 children, sc.

1. Catharine, wife of Daniel Hudson Esq. of St. Johns in the County of Roscommon.

2. Henry, who was curate of Kilkenny West, & left a son & Daughter at his Death, which happened 4 or 5 years ago. To this Brother the Traveller was inscribed.

3. Jane, wife of Mr. Johnson a farmer in Ireland.

4. Oliver, born at a Place called Pallas in the County of Longford in the Parish of Forney (a house belonging to his Wife's Uncle the Revd. Mr. Green Rector of Kilkenny West with whom his Father & Mother then resided.) He was born 29th Novr. 1731 (or 1730, h[4]

[1] "To England" is crossed out.

[2] On the opposite page, marked "Corrections from Dr. Goldsmith's Brother Maurice," is the following: "The Doctor's great grandfather Juan Romero came over to Ireland as private tutor to a Spanish Nobleman in the last Century, who was then on his travels."

[3] The correction reads, "A native of the County of Roscommon in the Diocese of Elphin at a place called Ballyoughter."

[4] "1731 (or 1730, h" is crossed out and "1728" added in the margin. This correction must have been Maurice's, since in the Memoir Percy

6. Charles, who went to Jamaica as a Cabinet Maker, where he now lives possessed of a good fortune.

5. Maurice, who lives now in Dublin a cabinet-maker.

7. John, who died young, circ. Aet. 12.

Th. Doctor's Mother died at Athlone, about 2 years & half ago.

The Doctor was educated chiefly under the Direction of his great Uncle Green, who placed him first at the Grammar School of Elphin[1] whence he removed him to Revd. Mr. Campbel's at Athlone, thence to Revd. Mr. Patrick Hughes's at Edgworthstown where he profitted more than any where, as the Master conversed with him on a footing very difft. from that of a young Scholar which the Doctor mentions with great gratitude & Respect. This Revd. Gentleman is still alive.

At 13[2] years of age he was entered at Dublin University under the Tuition of Theaker Wilder, who used him very harshly *and was a debauched licentious Man.*[3]

After taking the Degree of A.B. he proceeded upon the Line of Physic and took the Degree of M.B. when he was about 20, he however ceased to reside after his degree of A.B.[4]

While he was an undergraduate his Father died & left his family in distressed Circumstances, upon wch. the Revd.

offers "a member of Goldsmith's family" as authority for giving 1728 as the birth year.

[1] Here is added on the correction sheet, "under the Revd. Michl. Griffin."

[2] "Or 15 or 16" is added above.

[3] On the correction sheet opposite this statement is written, "He was rusticated from college for being concerned in a riot to set at large a Prisoner confined for Debt, who had been arrested within the Precincts of the College." The statement is made evidently on the authority of Thomas Wilson's letter to Malone, a copy of which is in the Meade collection.

[4] Percy has written here in the margin, "He most probably took no degree." The entire paragraph is bracketed, as if to express doubt.

Mr. Contarine,[1] who had mard. his Father's sister, took him under his care & finished his Education.

After his Degree of M.B.[2] (about 1751) he removed to Edinburgh[3] where he persued his Medical Studies under Monro for about 2 years and half, and then removed to Leiden where he staid about a year studying Chimistry under Gaubius & Anatomy under Albinus.

He then went (about 1753) *to Padua in Italy*,[4] where he staid 6 months & saw *Venice, Florence, Virona, & all the North Part of Italy*. His Uncle dying while he was at Padua,[5] he was obliged to return back thro France &c. on Foot, lodging at Convents chiefly of the Irish Nation. After spending in this perigrination near a year he came to settle in London this was about the breaking out of the War in 1756:—Here he first tried to practice Physic, living in the Bank Side, *& then removed to the Temple*:[6] where he had plenty of Patients, but got no Fees.

The Revd. Dr. Milner, a dissenting Minister of note, who kept a Classical School, at Peckham in Surrey, having a long fit of illness of which he soon after died, becoming acquainted with him thro' his son, who was also a young Physician, invited him to take the Care of his School During his illness, upon promise of securing him the Place of Chief Surgeon aboard an India-man: which promise he effectually fulfilled thro the Interest of Mr. Jones then a Director, the Doctor had accordingly made preparations for going abroad (in the

[1] Opposite is written, "Contryon or) Contarini."

[2] Above "his Degree of M.B." is written, "he left Dublin College," evidently as a substitute statement.

[3] Here is added on the opposite sheet, "at the expense of his Uncle Contarine who was like a Father to him."

[4] On the correction sheet opposite is written, "To Switzerland."

[5] "At Padua" is crossed out, and "thus abroad" substituted.

[6] The underlining of this shows that Percy doubted it, although he retained it in the Memoir. Proof of its veracity is found in an excised passage in Goldsmith's letter to his brother Henry, written in January 1758, in which he says, "I have taken chambers in the temple."

spring of 1757)[1] when happening to dine with Mr. Griffith the Bookseller, who was acquainted in Dr. Milner's Family, he was drawn into an agreemt. to write in his Review, in consideration of his board, Lodging, & *100 Pd. per annum.*[2] In this Thraldom[3] he lived 7 or 8 Months[4] Griffith and his wife continually objecting to everything he wrote & insisting on his implicitly submitting to their corrections [   ] & since Dr. Goldsmith lived with Griffith & his wife during this intercourse the Dr. and he[5] thought it incumbt. to drudge for his Pay constantly from 9 o'clock till 2. The above agreemt. (which was in writing) was to hold for a twelve-month, but by mutual consent was dissolved at the end of 7 or 8 months; when the Dr. removed into Green Arbour Court in the Old Bailey where he wrote his *Review of the Present State of Polite Literature in Europe printed for Dodsley* & published in 1759.[6] Here I first became acquainted with Dr. Goldsmith from supping along with him at the lodgings of our common Friend Dr. Grainger.

He afterwards removed to Lodgings at Mrs. Carnan's in Wine License Court Fleet Street: where he wrote his Vicar of Wakefield.

He then had Lodgings at Canonbury House Islington.

He afterwards Lodged up the Library Staircase in the Temple with Mr. Jeffs, the Butler of the Temple.

He then removed to Chambers of his own at No. 2 Brick Court in the Temple.

His Traveller was published about 1764.

His Deserted Village in 1770.

[1] Percy has written "9" under the last figure of the date.

[2] Over "*100 Pd. per annum*" is written, "some pecuniary stipend."

[3] "Thraldom" is excised, and "situation" substituted.

[4] From this point to "and he thought it incumbt," the writing is scratched over. The bracketed portion is illegible.

[5] "And he" is inserted to make the passage read smoothly, after the excision.

[6] Here two parallel lines are drawn, and seem to indicate where Goldsmith's dictation ends, and Percy's personal recollections begin.

N.B. Mr. Boswell says he had lodgings in the King's Bench Walk in the Temple in 1766, Feb.

Goldsmith also handed to Percy, at some unspecified time, a packet of letters and papers of a miscellaneous nature, "without," as Percy later wrote to Steevens, "much inquiry from me at the time, or explanation from him."[1] The date must, however, have been approximately the same as the date of the dictation of the Memorandum, since all the documents the packet contains date from 1771, 1772, and 1773. The only use Percy made of it was to reprint three of the letters it contained—the begging letter from John Oakman, and those from General Oglethorpe and Tom Paine, in the Memoir, and to add the two rejected epilogues for *She Stoops to Conquer*, found therein, to the Collected Poems. The other documents in it, unused by Percy but still remaining in the collection inherited by Miss Meade, relate almost entirely to the production of *She Stoops to Conquer*, and include letters from Chambers, the architect, Lord Charlemont, Mrs Bulkley, and others, as well as the letter from Colman asking to be taken "off the rack of the newspapers." The miscellaneous character of the contents, and the trifling nature of some of them, indicate clearly that Goldsmith exercised no principle of selection, but merely collected the contents of his desk and handed them over, to supplement the meagre account of himself dictated to Percy. In April, 1773, letters relating to his play would naturally predominate. It is worth

[1] Nichols, *Illust.* VII, 31.

noting that what appears to be a portion of this same collection, consisting of letters addressed to Goldsmith, dating from 1773, from Murphy, Cumberland, Mrs Thrale, and others, became detached from the original collection, some time in the nineteenth century, and was offered for sale by William Evarts Benjamin of New York in March, 1886. Since they were offered with a group of letters addressed to Dr and Mrs Percy, it seems obvious that they must have formed part of the Goldsmithiana in Percy's possession. Their present location I have been unable to ascertain.

After Goldsmith's death, on April 4, 1774, all his friends seem to have combined to salvage what they could of the facts of his life. A letter from Lady P. Knight written on April 18 to Goldsmith's Edinburgh friend, Dr William Farr, after mentioning the circumstances of Goldsmith's death, adds:

She [Miss Francis Reynolds] tells me they are exceedingly Puzzled to know what Dr. Goldsmith followd when he first came to town and how he was educated &c. and I belive they intend makeing aplication to you for to be helpt out with some Materials for writing his Life. . . . [1]

Apparently, however, Farr was not called into service at this time; but for the curious way in which his knowledge of Goldsmith's life was finally utilized in the Memoir, the reader may turn to the end of this history. Beside Reynolds, Garrick also offered his services, as the letter from Maurice Goldsmith, quoted below, shows. But there is no doubt that

[1] B.M. Add. MS. 37060.

Percy continued to regard himself as the actual biographer. When Maurice Goldsmith came to London to settle the estate of his brother, Percy commissioned him to collect all the available information about his brother upon his return to Ireland. Acting on these instructions, and in a glow of hope that at last he was to gain some tangible benefit from his brother's fame, Maurice collected that famous group of early letters which were first published in the Memoir, and, in addition, got his sister, Mrs Hodson, to write that account of Goldsmith's boyhood which is usually referred to as the "Hodson narrative." A letter from Maurice to Percy, preserved in the Meade collection, dated July 15, 1776, reveals the circumstances:

Revd. Sir,

When I last had the honour of seeing you at your Chambers in Northumberland House you most kindly told me you wod willingly serve me. I have Sir according to your Order collected in this Country all the Letters and a few anecdotes of my Brother, the late Docter Goldsmith that I cod procure which I assure you Sir are entirely Jenuine, the Anecdotes wrote by his Sister who ware both inseperable Companions in their youth.

I am much concernd that two of these Letters which I send are not entirely Legibl and that it will cost som pains to mak them and the Memoirs fitt for the press; So Dr Sir to your goodness and protection I commit them thoroughly satisfied you will serve the Brother of a Man who really lovd and Esteemd you.

I can assure you Sir I have gon several Miles to Collect them and as my Circumstances at present are not verry Affluent a small assistance wod be gratefully accepted, shd. any accrue from these papers wich with what my good Friend Sr. Josshua Reynolds and Mr. Garrick promisd to supply, will not be deemd I hope unworthy of yr publication which you and Sir Josshua told me you wod get affected.

I am Sir with the gratest respect Sir your verry Obet. Humble Servant

Maurice Goldsmith

I hope you will do me the honour to let me know if you receivd these by directing to me at Charles Town near Elphin Ireland.

Another bit of evidence that Percy had not relinquished to Johnson his intention of writing the Life as late as 1775 is found in a diary of Dr Thomas Campbell, who later became Percy's collaborator in the Memoir. In recording a conversation he had with Percy and Johnson in April, 1775, he says, "When Dr. Goldsmith was mentioned, and Dr. Percy's intention of writing his life, he [Johnson] expressed his approbation strongly."[1]

Johnson evidently claimed the office of biographer some time in 1776, the exact date being uncertain. An undated letter from Maurice Goldsmith to Dr Johnson "at his house in Bolt Court Fleet Street London," preserved in the Percy collection, reveals that after his letter of July 15, 1776, to Percy, the latter had informed him of the shift of responsibility to his more venerable friend. It reads:

I lately had the Honour to receive a letter from my good Friend the Revd. Docr. Percy, who from som Papers I had sent him did intend writing the life of the Late Docr. Gold-

[1] "Diary of a Visit to England by Dr Thomas Campbell" in Napier, *Johnsoniana*, 1884.

THE HISTORY OF THE MEMOIR

smith: he tells me that from the esteem you have had for the poor Docr. you have determind to take the work under your protection and that you had also promised to use your interest with the booksellers.... Your taking the trouble to write and set of the life of the Docr. by your able judicious and highly esteemed pen will be a lasting honour to his memory and his Family.[1]

As late as June, 1776, Percy had certainly not yet relinquished the task, since at that time Johnson sent the "poor dear Doctor's" epitaph to Reynolds, without either the date or place of Goldsmith's birth included, and said in his note, "The dates must be settled by Dr. Percy."[2] If the materials for the biography had already been turned over, such a procedure would not have been necessary.

It is certain, however, that by February, 1777, Johnson was launched on his task. A Mrs Goldsmith, in all probability the widow of Henry, visited London some time during that winter, and was commissioned by Johnson, as her brother-in-law had been previously by Percy, to collect data concerning Goldsmith's life in Ireland. On February 25 he wrote George Steevens:

You will be glad to hear that from Mrs. Goldsmith, whom we lamented as drowned, I have received a letter full of gratitude to us all, with promise to make the enquiries which we recommended to her.[3]

Another active step which Johnson took was to secure from Malone, who was at that time resident in

[1] Clarke, *Trans. Bib. Soc.* xv, 51. This letter has disappeared since Clarke's examination of the collection.
[2] Boswell, *Life of Johnson,* ed. Hill, III, 81.
[3] *Ibid.* p. 100.

Ireland, a letter dated February 24, 1776, which had been sent him by Dr Wilson, fellow of Trinity College, Dublin, recording the facts about Goldsmith's college career which could be gleaned from the college records. Malone undoubtedly secured this letter primarily for use in the Memoir with which he prefaced the edition of Goldsmith's poems which he published in Dublin in 1777, although he later said, in a note to his edition of Boswell's *Life of Johnson*,[1] that he had secured it at Dr Johnson's desire.

It is well known how Johnson's attempt to write the Life, and edit the works, of his friend was balked. Carnan, the partner of Francis Newbery, and owner of the copyright of *She Stoops to Conquer*, invoked the newly-passed copyright law to refuse permission for the reprinting of that play. It is not clear whether he opposed the separate edition which Johnson at first planned, or whether he opposed its inclusion among the *Works of the English Poets*, projected by the forty eminent booksellers of London in March, 1777, for which Johnson was engaged to write the biographical prefaces—the modest beginning of the *Lives of the Poets*. The effect, however, was the same. The copyright law protected Carnan until 1787, fourteen years after the first publication of the play, and as the Life could not, according to their eighteenth-century point of view, avail much without the works, there was nothing to do but wait. Johnson died before the time had expired. There is no reason

[1] Boswell, *Life of Johnson*, ed. Hill, III, 100, note 1.

to suppose, however, that had he lived he would not have resumed the task at the expiration of the copyright. Malone, who seems to have known more about Johnson's plans for the Life than anyone else, wrote to Percy on March 2, 1785 (the letter is quoted in full below), "Dr. Johnson used to say that he never could get an accurate account of Goldsmith's history while he was abroad," which seems to indicate a continued effort on Johnson's part to collect information on the subject. It is not necessary to point out that Percy was misinformed, in accusing Johnson, in his reply to Malone, of utterly forgetting both Goldsmith's family and the Memoir.

Upon Johnson's death a curious accident brought back the materials for the Memoir into Percy's hands. By this time, of course, he had been elevated to the see of Dromore, in Ireland, having been consecrated bishop on April 20, 1782. Malone, in London, had requested Dr Scott, one of Johnson's executors, to return to him the letter of Dr Wilson, already referred to, which he had given to Johnson eight years before. The letter he wrote to Percy on the subject on March 2, 1785, remains in Miss Meade's collection:

I suppose Dr. Scott, to whom I talked on the subject, did not exactly recollect what I had mentioned, for about a fortnight ago, a parcel of papers was sent to me marked at the outside "Dr. Goldsmith," as I imagine from the executors (for I received no note from them), who conceived they belonged to me. On inspecting them, I found they consisted of some very curious materials collected by your Lordship for the life of Goldsmith, which I shall take great care of till I hear from you on the subject. I often pressed Dr. Johnson to write his life, and he would have done so, had not the booksellers from some clashing of interests in the property of his works excluded them from their great collection of English Poetry. It is a great pity that these materials should be lost. Why will not your lordship, who knew Goldsmith so well, undertake the arranging of them. Dr. Wilson's letter relative to Goldsmith's being rusticated for rescuing one of his college friends from Newgate, I suppose perished in the general destruction that Johnson made of his papers a little before he died. But Dr. Wilson is now alive, and in the University of Dublin, and will readily communicate whatever he knows. Dr. J. used to say that he never could get an accurate account of Goldsmith's history while he was abroad. There is a person now in Dublin who knows a great deal of that history, having studied physick with him at Leyden,— Dr. Ellis who is now Clerk of the house of Commons. He was in a very ill state of health when I saw him about a year ago; so that it would be prudent to get this history from him as soon as may be. Our friend Lord Charlemont, I believe, knows him and would interest himself about it. Goldsmith's letters are surely characteristick and worth preserving.

Percy readily resumed the office thus reintrusted to him, and on June 1, even before he had answered Malone's letter, he issued proposals for a subscription edition of Goldsmith's poems:

Dublin, June 1, 1785.

Proposals For Printing by Subscription, The Poetical Works of Dr. Oliver Goldsmith; For the Benefit of his Only Surviving Brother, Mr. Maurice Goldsmith. To Which Will be Prefixed, A New Life Of The Author. In this will be Corrected Innumerable Errors of Former Biographers, From Original Letters of the Doctor and his Friends; But Chiefly From An Account of Dr. Goldsmith's Life, Dictated by Himself to a Gentleman Who is in Possession of the Manuscript. Dublin: Printed for H. Whitestone, W. Wilson, R. Moncrieffe, C. Jenkin, R. Burton, and R. Marchbank.

He evidently had not received the packet from Malone, who was holding it pending advice from him, when these were issued, and he was therefore depending on a nine-year-old memory of what it contained.

He associated Dr Barnard, Bishop of Killaloe, a member of the Club and former friend of Goldsmith, with him in this enterprise, but that worthy seems to have taken no active part. Shortly afterwards he replied to Malone, in a letter which has been printed both by Prior and Nichols. It is dated June 16, 1785, and, after expressing gratitude for the recovery of the papers, relates how they came into the Doctor's possession, and berates him for his careless forgetfulness, citing as evidence that he "gave a wrong place for that of his [Goldsmith's] birth—*Elphin*, which is accordingly so sculptured in Westminster Abbey." He then adds: "Dr. Wilson's very curious letter, which you thought lost, I have happily in my possession, so that we may readily compile a good, at least a correct, account of the principal events of Dr. Goldsmith's life; and, with the assistance of one or other of his friends, may be able to fill up an account for almost all the time he spent from his leaving Edinburgh till he rose into public notice."[1] He

[1] This passage of the letter is printed in Nichols' *Illust.* VIII, 239, as a separate fragment, and dated, erroneously, "About 1788." How Percy came into possession of the Wilson letter, whether from Dr Johnson's executors, or from the Doctor himself before his death, is not known. A copy of it, not in Percy's hand, remains in Miss Meade's collection.

closes with an account of the projected edition for the benefit of Maurice, urging Malone to solicit the help of the Club, with the assistance of Reynolds and Steevens. The Proposals themselves were not sent over until July 3, in care of Malone's brother, Lord Sunderlin. Percy's accompanying letter, now in the collection of Mr R. B. Adam of Buffalo, contains several allusions to Maurice and the proposed edition:

Herewith I send you an original Begging Letter, which I must desire to have returned: a Copy of it, you wd. have hardly thought genuine.... Along with Goldsmith's Proposals I send a Poetic Effort from this Country for our new Poet Laureate & will beg your kind assistance to convey it to him.... I was just sealing up this wh[en] I was favoured with a Letter fro[m] Sir Joshua Reynolds dated June 25. In it he kindly promises to serve Mr. M. Goldsmith (for after I wrote the inclosed to you, I mentioned it to Sr. J. R.) If Mrs. Montagu sees the poor Man's Letter I know it will prevent any further solicitation: and therefore when you have made what use you think convent. pray give it Sr J[oshua] to show it to her...."

The expected aid from Mrs Montagu was evidently not so great as Percy expected, for he continued his requests for help from the Club, suggesting a guinea apiece as a suitable contribution. Finally, in April, 1787, he reported to Malone that Maurice had secured a "snug little place in the License Office."[1]

The progress of the edition itself was slow. Percy learned from Malone, in a letter dated September 28, 1786,[2] of the recalcitrance of Carnan; and the know-

---

[1] Nichols, *Illust.* VIII, 238.
[2] Prior, I, p. xi.

ledge that his Dublin edition would be opposed as a piracy by the London publisher was probably what led him to defer it until the copyright should be liberated in England, in 1787. The complete transference of the publication from Dublin to London does not seem to have taken place, however, until after January 11, 1788, for on that date a letter[1] from George Steevens to Percy shows that just previously Percy had sent him a copy of the Dublin Proposals, and he adds that he "hopes the expiration of the copyright will soon afford scope for [Percy's] supplemental charity," by which the responsibility of the copyright for delaying the edition is clearly indicated. Percy occupied the enforced interval by enlarging the original scope of the plan to include Goldsmith's prose works, and then by efforts to collect the scattered unpublished fragments of his prose. The original suggestion for the enlargement of the plan came from Malone, as is shown by the following excerpt from Percy's letter of October 17, 1786, to Malone, now in Mr R. B. Adam's collection:

I am quite pleased with the hint of taking into our intended Publications of Goldsmith's Pieces, the Prose-Compositions wch. you mention and shall desire you to collect & arrange them for our Volume. I wish you could get me one or two things of his wch. were never published: viz. His Prospectus or Plan of his Dictionary of Arts and Sciences: a kind of Memoir, wch. he drew up about the beginning of the present Reign, wch. he offered to Lord Bute, proposing to travel into the interior parts of India: A paper wch. he wrote to set about a Subscription for poor Smart the mad poet:

[1] Nichols, *Illust.* VII, 4.

(I believe this last was never printed.) All these things, I believe might be got from Mr. Bott, sometime of the Temple, who was his principal Creditor & took possession of all his Papers. These with the Letters you mention & any others, that could be procured, wd. be valuable accessions.

Thus began the first effort to collect and reprint Goldsmith's prose, which, in the opinion of many modern critics, is the most important basis of his fame; but this almost accidental inclusion of it helps to prove that it was tardily recognized and completely under-rated by his contemporaries. Dr Johnson should be noted, however, as an exception. As to the lost works mentioned in the letter, Malone evidently failed to locate them, and Percy later commissioned the indefatigable Boswell to do so. Boswell wrote to Percy on March 12, 1790, "I am in the way of getting at many additional works of his which I shall communicate to your Lordship."[1] (What these works were, or whether Boswell subsequently sent them, is not known.) He failed, also, in the hunt for the *Prospectus*, and informed Percy of the fact on April 9, 1790.[2]

In the meantime, Percy had definitely decided to bring out the edition in London, and opened negotiations with the well-known printer and publisher, John Nichols. The agreement was never consummated, although it is difficult to understand why, in view of Nichols' generous concession to all Percy's terms. A letter of July 2, 1789, from Nichols to

---

[1] *Letters of James Boswell*, ed. C. B. Tinker, II, 392.
[2] *Ibid.* 394. The Plan has never been recovered.

Percy, states the terms which Percy at first laid down, which turned out, singularly enough, to be precisely the same terms as those finally made after a long period of haggling with the United Booksellers. Nichols' early connection with the Edition has not before been noticed. The letter reads:

For the other part of your letter, I shall be happy in any way to be the instrument of serving Mr. Goldsmith. I will print the work, if your Lordship thinks proper, *meo periculo* every way. Under your Lordship's assistance I will be the ostensible editor, and I will furnish Mr. Goldsmith gratis with 250 copies for his subscribers; and with more, (if he wants them) at a moderate price. The whole, therefore, now waits only for your Lordship's further directions. The secret of your Lordship's share in the Biography, or as Editor, shall be preserved; and the fame of the deceased, and emolument of his surviving brother, be consulted as much as in the power of, my Lord, your Lordship's servant, etc.[1]

This letter gives the first evidence of Percy's strange prejudice against allowing his name to be connected with the edition. This shunning of publicity marked all the later literary ventures of the Bishop's life,[2] and can be explained only on the grounds that Ritson's recent attack on the *Reliques* had not only morbidly offended Percy, but had intimidated him as well. The letter also reflects that characteristic "regard for the fame of the deceased" which

---

[1] Nichols, *Illust.* VIII, 82.

[2] In publishing his *Specimens of Blank Verse before Milton*, Percy used his nephew as ostensible editor, as he did also for the fourth volume of the *Reliques*. This subterfuge is the subject for much jest by George Steevens, in his correspondence with Percy in 1796–7. (Nichols, *Illust.* VII, 5–36.)

prompted his unjustified tampering with the texts of the letters, and his resentment at some of Rose's interpolations later.

The "ostensible" biographer upon whom Percy's choice lighted was the Rev. Thomas Campbell, rector of Clones, in Ireland, with whom he had been acquainted at least since 1775, as has been pointed out, and who had already interested himself in Goldsmith in his *Philosophical Survey of the South of Ireland*, published in 1777. His active work on it seems to have lasted from about April, 1790, until the spring of 1792, and it must be made clear, in order that one may understand the apparent dilatoriness of both Percy and Campbell, that during that entire period they managed to meet only once, some time before the spring of 1791, for consultation. Campbell was writing almost entirely from the documents and recollections of Percy, as he himself had never known Goldsmith, and he had no available resources for research. Percy discovered an additional cause for delay: he could not conclude an agreement with a London publisher without being on the spot, and a sense of duty to his office, as well as the illness of Mrs Percy, kept him continually in Ireland from the time of his elevation in 1782 until the spring of 1791.[1]

Campbell's correspondence[2] with Percy during these years gives a clear idea of the materials he worked into the Memoir. It will be noted in the

[1] Gaussen, *Percy, Prelate and Poet*, p. 245.
[2] Nichols, *Illust.* VII, 777–790.

following digest of the correspondence that the bulk of the writing was completed by September, 1790, and the continuance of Campbell's connection with it was caused by the delay in meeting Percy for a final settlement and revision. The items which were excluded from the Memoir in its final form are marked with an asterisk.

April 6, 1790:
  *Has sketched an Exordium to the Life, and wants to include mention of Percy's share, and the "number of copies Nichols is to give."

May 20, 1790:
  Asks for *Present State of Polite Learning*, which he has not read.

June 16, 1790:
  Has Goldsmith in London and is endeavouring to recollect the story of the "loan...of the chamber pot of coals."
  Has defended Goldsmith against the attacks of Sir John Hawkins.
  Desires a copy of *She Stoops to Conquer*, which he has not read.
  *Desires the MS. notes to the *Present State of Polite Learning* which Percy had promised him.
  *Asks for more information about the Perrot-Goldsmith story.

June 30, 1790:
  Has missed seeing Percy at Armagh because of Mrs Percy's illness.
  Has received "your picture of Green Arbor court," which shall be "closely copied." (This is the chamber-pot of coals story.)
  Has received the story of Johnson's first visit to Goldsmith.

*"The story of the valet de chambre will, as Lord Bristol says, pin the basket of his absurdities, and really we may have a hamper full of them."

Asks for the chronology of Goldsmith's connection with Newbery.

*Declares his intention of including the account of Griffiths' altering Goldsmith's reviews for the *Monthly*.[1]

*Promises that the story of Sir Richard Perrot will not appear to come from Percy.

Says he will return *Parnell's Life*, since he has a copy.

August 3, 1790:

Thanks Percy for the second volume of Goldsmith,—the plays.

Has not written a line of Goldsmith "this month and more."

September 9, 1790:

Declares he can finish the Life *currente prelo*.

Is having difficulty in having it transcribed so that Percy can read it.

Regrets that Mrs Percy's illness makes uncertain their time for setting out for England, where Campbell had intended delivering the papers and receiving Percy's alterations and amendments.

*Has made "large quotations here and there from Goldsmith's own works."

Has drawn a parallel between Addison's *Letter from Italy* and that part of the *Traveller* which refers to it.

*Has defended the *Deserted Village* "upon facts and principles of Dr. Price," and has "drawn some political consequences respecting this my poor native country, and...mounted my hobby horse in defending a union."

---

[1] This account formed part of Percy's MS. Memorandum of Goldsmith's Life (*q.v.*) but was scored out, evidently at a later date. Griffiths was still alive at this time.

The next letter is dated August 13, 1791, and in the interval, Campbell had seen Percy at Dromore, and the Bishop had indicated in the MS. the alterations he wished. The MS. preserved in this state was examined by Prior, who describes it in his Preface, without stating in whose possession it was at the time. The Bishop and his family departed for England in the spring of 1791, and were residing at Bath for Mrs Percy's health. An arrangement for Percy and Campbell to meet in London and launch the publication, was thwarted by Campbell's being delayed by a lawsuit in Dublin. The letter of August 13, 1791, makes this clear, and contains a further promise to meet Percy in England in November. This plan, too, was thwarted, as Campbell's letter of January 5, 1792, reveals, because he was delayed again in Dublin, and had to hurry home on account of the near approach of Christmas. On February 3 he wrote again, making a third appointment to meet his patron in England in the middle of the month, and proposing to carry the unaltered sheets to London, and spend March there "printing off the first sheets and sending the proofs to you at Bath," making the proposed alterations "for the immediate press copy, with which I could wish to furnish the printer, not altogether but as he shall want it; so that while I am inserting such circumstances as seem rightly stated by Boswell,[1] and writing it out fair, the printer may be going on with

---

[1] Boswell's *Life of Johnson*, which had come out in the preceding year, is referred to.

the beginning, in which you think no alterations, but such as you have noted, need be made." From this letter it seems clear that both Campbell and Percy regarded the Memoir as practically ready for publication at this time, nor is there any reason for supposing that Percy was dissatisfied with Campbell's work. Clarke assumed that Percy took the work out of his hands because he had not known Goldsmith personally.[1] The real explanation, however, is that at this point a delay occurred over the printing, and, before that matter could be satisfactorily arranged, Campbell died. His death, which seems never to have been noted in accounts of the Memoir, took place on June 20, 1795.[2]

The delay in the printing was occasioned by a shift from Nichols to Murray, probably shortly before June 12, 1793, for on that date Campbell wrote to him from Clones, "I am glad you have brought the affair of Goldsmith to so good an issue." The employment of Murray is rather vaguely noted by Prior, who says:

The late Mr. Murray of Fleet-Street was first[3] selected for publisher of Goldsmith's Works, but he died during the negociation. A few letters of Malone to Bishop Percy, still extant, state the circumstances.[4]

Murray died on November 6, 1793,[5] just three

[1] *Trans. Bib. Soc.* xv, 16–17.
[2] Nichols, *Illust.* vii, 795.
[3] Prior did not know of Nichols' early connection as prospective publisher.
[4] I, p. xiv, and note.
[5] Timperley, *Encyclopedia of Literary and Typographical Anecdote*, p. 781.

months after Percy had returned to Ireland from his
two-years' stay in England, and Percy did not find
opportunity to return to England, and to open
negotiations with another publisher, until 1794,
upon the death of his cousin, William Cleveland,
whose heir he was.[1] The administration of his cousin's
estate, and other business, prevented attention to the
matter of the edition until the end of 1795. In the
meantime, Campbell had died, and Percy was accordingly under the necessity of finding a new "ostensible"
editor, as well as a new publisher.

In the autumn of 1795, Percy opened negotiations
with the united booksellers of London, represented
by Cadell and Davies. The portion of the Memoir's
history most difficult to unravel is the ensuing period,
with its attendant misunderstandings, ending with a
complete break between the editor and the publishers,
and the final appearance of the edition, in the spring
of 1802, under the nominal editorship of Samuel
Rose. A portion of Percy's correspondence with
Cadell and Davies has, however, recently been re-
trieved and this clears up most of the doubtful points.
Two especially significant documents have, unfortunately, not been recovered. The first of these is an
account which Percy transmitted to Anderson and
Malone in 1807, and to which he refers, in an unpublished letter, written to Malone on May 26,
1808, and preserved in the Bodleian,[2] as a "statement

---

[1] Gaussen, *Percy, Prelate and Poet*, p. 237.
[2] MS. Malone 39.

of what passed between him and Messrs. Cadell and Davies on the subject of Dr. Goldsmith's Life, which he drew up for their edition of his Miscellaneous Works in 4 vols. 8vo, and which they had interpolated and altered, and even refused to let him see his own manuscript; afterwards publishing in vindication of their misconduct a gross misrepresentation of the whole transaction." The second missing document is this vindication of Cadell and Davies, which must have appeared in some periodical of the day, but which I have been unable to locate.

The original source of the misunderstanding seems to have been the fact that there were two distinct sets of terms proposed in the winter of 1795–6, the first by the booksellers, on November 6, 1795, and the second by Percy, on January 4, 1796. Each side considered, or affected to consider, that its terms had been accepted; and, although Percy was emphatically disillusioned on this point in the summer of 1797, when the negotiations were reopened, and, although he at that time acceded without reservations to the terms then insisted upon by the publishers, he was not able to relinquish the idea that he had been unfairly treated, nor to forbear advancing his own terms again, in 1800. This final act caused the irritated publishers to make their final break with him.

The terms proposed by the booksellers on November 6, 1795, were recorded in the books of the Chapter Coffee House, and Malone took the trouble, the next year, when the agreement was again being agitated, to look them up and call Percy's attention to the fact that their offer was "exactly on the terms they now offer."[1] This offer was 250 copies in sheets to be sold in Ireland, with no mention of an immediate money payment to the relatives. Percy's counter-proposals, the date of which is stated in the same unpublished letter to Malone, quoted above, were 200 guineas for Esther and Catherine Goldsmith, sixty copies for former subscribers, and thirty guineas for having the Life rewritten.[2] He remained in England until the summer of 1796, without, however, closing with the publishers on either set of terms, being mainly engaged in collecting specimens of blank verse before Milton, which he later published. He returned to find Ireland in the throes of alarm over a French invasion and Catholic uprising. In spite of the turmoil of his domestic and official life, he found time to delegate his friend, the Rev. Henry Boyd, to rewrite the Memoir, for which service he paid him thirty guineas from his own pocket. An unpublished letter from Percy to Cadell and Davies, now the property of Mr Harold Murdock, of Boston, Massachusetts, throws light on the question of the extent of Boyd's contribution to the Memoir:

Dublin, March 27, 1797.

Gentlemen,

On my coming to Dublin, in February last, I had an interview with Mr. Boyd, the ingenious translator of Dante, and proposed to him the completion of Dr. Goldsmith's Life

---

[1] Nichols, *Illust.* VII, 28–9.
[2] See the letter to Cadell and Davies of July 26, 1797, quoted below.

which he readily undertook, and I was to have seen him here again (for he lives at some distance from Dublin) about the 17th Inst. with the Whole or a considerable part of it executed. Under this expectation I delayed writing to you: but being informed today by a Letter that he had been indisposed, yet had nearly completed the Undertaking, which he hoped erelong to show me, I would not delay writing to you any longer to convince you that I have not been inattentive either to the Public, Dr. Goldsmith's Family or his Publishers. I have the honour to be

> Gentlemen,
>> Your obedient
>>> humble servant,
>>>> Thos. Dromore.

It seems apparent, from the brief time originally allowed him, that Boyd was not expected to do more than incorporate into Campbell's text Percy's corrections made in 1791. His only active contribution to the Memoir appears to have been an attempt to confirm Dr Wilson's account of Goldsmith's college career, by communicating with John Kearney, a fellow of Trinity College, Dublin. A letter to Boyd from Kearney, dated June 16, 1797, preserved among Percy's papers, adds nothing to Wilson's account except the names of the students expelled for the Newgate delivery, and of those censured with Goldsmith. He adds that a search of the records fails to show that Goldsmith ever received an A.B.—a fact which is duly mentioned in the Memoir. Boyd certainly brought in no other new material of his own; and it is somewhat difficult to see how he earned thirty guineas by his labours. It is certain, from

Anderson's letter to Percy, of June 3, 1805, quoted below, that the publishers regarded the "bringing-in of Boyd" as one of Percy's most objectionable deeds.

Boyd had just finished his delayed task when Percy again set out for England to visit his newly-married daughter, Mrs Isted, in the spring of 1797. On July 26 he wrote Cadell and Davies a letter[1] in which, as has already been pointed out, he ignored the publishers' terms, and reiterated his own, using as coercion the unpublished works of Goldsmith in his possession, without which, of course, the publishers could not secure a renewed copyright to the *Works*. The letter reads:

Near Northampton, July 26, 1797.

Gentlemen,

The business which brought me over from Ireland in the Spring has never once allowed me to come to London, as I expected; this alone has prevented me from seeing you on the subject of Dr. Goldsmith's works as I proposed: and the advance of summer &c makes it now less likely that I shd. soon visit the Metropolis. Yet as I shd. be sorry to occasion you & the Proprietors further inconvenience by my absence, I submit to you, whether the Treaty might not be brought to some Conclusion between us by Letter: so that you may at once begin to print your proposed Edition. I shall be contented for the Terms formerly proposed by me, to let you have all the Materials for the intended Improvements.—

The Terms I proposed, were 200 guineas for the Niece and Sister in Law of the Author, with about 60 Copies to supply Demands of former subscribers, when it was intended

[1] This letter, now in the collection of Mr R. B. Adam of Buffalo, has not hitherto been published.

to print the work by Subscription. And 30 guineas for Mr. Boyd for writing the author's *Life*, wch. I have actually paid him out of my own pocket, as he cd. not wait.the delay of a Negotiation.

For the above sums will be delivered to the Proprietors of Dr. Goldsmith's former works: 2 Poems, wch. so far as I know & believe were never printed being two Epilogues of considerable Length; & a great number of Original Letters which shall be introduced into the Life.—

If you approve of the above Terms, and will propose proper articles of Agreemt. to be signed on both sides, (half the Money to be paid now & the Remainder when the new Edition is printed off) your proposed edition may be set to press, and if the plan of it is communicated to me I will suggest all possible Improvements, so far as I can at this Distance. But I would recommend the printing of the *Life* to be reserved till the last, that it may receive my latest Recollections, even if I am not repaid the Money I advanced to Mr. Boyd, till the *Life* go to the Press.

In all this I have no Desire of Advantage to myself & only wish to serve the poor Women for whom I have indeed already procured assistance from our Governmt. so that they will not suffer by any delay: Thus you & the proprietors may act as you please & I shall remain at all events, Gentlemen

Your obedient humble Servant

Thomas Dromore.

Their reply has not been preserved, but we know, from Percy's letter to George Steevens on September 6, printed below, that they rejected his terms, and reiterated their own. To this letter, Percy sent a smoothly acquiescent reply on August 30, the pertinent passages of which read:

In your proposed terms of agreement I have little objection, only before I engage for the Epilogue having been never printed, I have applied to a friend much more conversant with the stage than I am, to make a very minute search into that subject. The longest and most valuable of the two, which I have in the Doctor's own handwriting, I have every reason to believe never was, and this will be sufficient to secure to the proprietors a renewed property in his Works. The other he gave me in a packet of his letters and papers, but being in the handwriting of the actor who was to recite it, may have got into some old magazine, though I never heard it was in any.

Mr. Boyd had just finished his Life of Goldsmith as I was leaving Ireland, and I have been too much engaged with more important business since I came over to give it a regular revisal; but from a cursory inspection I see that, although it is elegantly written, yet as I knew personally and intimately Dr. Goldsmith, which Mr. Boyd did not, I can exceedingly improve it, which I am willing to do gratis, and with as much speed as is consistent with my health and other more important engagements...not to mention other avocations. ...If you can send me all the copies from which you intend to print, I will give them a previous revision, and can perhaps supply some illustrations. If you accept the proposal, I will in my next direct you how to send them to

Your obedient servant.[1]

Percy had meanwhile, as his letter indicates, written to his friend, George Steevens, to search for the second epilogue. (The two epilogues in question were—although neither Percy, Steevens, nor the proprietors of the *Works* recognized the fact—the two epilogues which Goldsmith first wrote and rejected for *She Stoops to Conquer*.) An exchange of six

[1] Nichols, *Illust.* VIII, 672.

B   6

letters[1] took place, the most significant of which is Percy's of September 6, in which he states the book-sellers' terms, and expresses his indignation:

I wish to consult you about an answer I am about to send to a captious letter of Messrs. Cadell and Davies, who have been in treaty for what *Reliques* I have of Goldsmith; which I want to make advantageous to two poor women nearly related to him. When I was last in England I had reason to expect they would give me 200 guineas for them in money, and 50 copies of a proposed edition in four vols. as also repay me twenty or thirty guineas for a Life, which I was to have written by some man of character....Since my return to England, Messrs. Cadell and Davies...utterly refused to pay any money for the poor women (though they did not refuse to pay me my thirty guineas): but proposed, as soon as the four vols. of this collected edition of Dr. Goldsmith's works is completed, to "supply to the order of the Bishop of Dromore 250 perfect sets, in sheets, of the said edition, free of all charge, for the purpose of the said sets being sent to Ireland and disposed of in that kingdom, for the benefit of two sur-viving relations of Dr. Goldsmith." Knowing that the poor women would not be able to dispose of them unless I went about soliciting subscriptions through that kingdom, which I cannot now submit to, and that our Irish booksellers would some of them get their books and never pay them, I desired they would leave out the condition of the *books being all to be disposed of in Ireland*; and allow them in part to be sold here. They now will admit of no other alternative but either my sending the 250 copies in sheets to Ireland, with the carriage at my own expense, there to be stitched or bound,

---

[1] Percy's first letter is not preserved; Steevens' reply, of Sept. 3, is in Nichols, *Illust.* VII, 24; Percy's reply, of Sept. 6, was printed in the *Athenæum*, April 29, 1848; Steevens' reply, of Sept. 9, is in Nichols, *Illust.* VII, 28; Percy's reply of Sept. 10, is in Nichols, *Illust.* VII, 31; and Steevens' reply, of Sept. 14, is in Nichols, *Illust.* VII, 32.

and sold, etc.—or else they will give me here only 200 copies
for them, stitched in blue paper, with liberty to dispose of
them in England. This proposal is made in terms so uncivil,
that I think they wish me to be affronted, and so break off
all further treaty; which I should really prefer, with the loss of
my thirty guineas, but for the sake of the poor women, etc.[1]

Although some further exchange of letters had undoubtedly followed Percy's letter of August 30 to
Cadell and Davies, the tenor of the agreement could
hardly have been materially changed thereby. We
find the bishop, then, assuring the publishers in one
breath, "in your proposed terms of agreement I have
little objection," and in the next complaining bitterly
to Steevens of their injustice. The exasperation of the
booksellers with Percy's manner of doing business
is comprehensible after one has traced him through
such a timid contradiction as this.

Steevens' reply to this letter has already been
referred to. It is the one pointing out that the terms
on the Chapter Coffee House books for November 6,
1795, were identical with those now offered by the
booksellers.

The final agreement, which conceded to Percy the
privilege of 250 copies, one-half of which could be
sold in England, was reached shortly afterwards.[2]
The privilege of revising the Life at his leisure was
certainly accorded him, as he requested, for we find
him writing to Cadell and Davies on the eve of his

---

[1] *Athenæum*, April 29, 1848.
[2] For the terms in full see Percy's letter to Nichols, in *Illust.*
VI, 583.

departure for Ireland the next spring—April 6, 1798:

I should have sent you the copy of Dr. Goldsmith's Life, etc. last week as I proposed, but my journey to Ireland being delayed till next week, I have employed the intervening time in giving it a thorough revisal. I shall send it the beginning of next week, and with it some of his fugitive pieces, which till now have not been known to be his; as also a new and beautiful stanza of the *Hermit*, which will render all former editions of that poem incomplete and defective.... [1]

Two unpublished letters of Percy to Cadell and Davies, written from Ireland shortly after his return, have come to light, the first in the possession of Mr Harold Murdock, of Boston, and the second in that of Mr W. M. Elkins, of Philadelphia. They both bear eloquent witness to the publishers' compliance with Percy's request to revise his manuscript, a privilege which Percy later twice accused them of denying him, once in the unpublished letter to Malone of May 26, 1808, quoted above, and again in a letter to Nichols, of May 19, 1802, which will be noticed later. The first is dated from Dublin, June 2, 1798, and reads:

Gentlemen,

Since I sent you the sheets of the Manuscript Life of Goldsmith I have received some material information which I wish to insert in its proper place. Be so good therefore as to look in that part, which relates to his residence at Leyden, and subsequent travels in Switzerland, and either copy so much of it as relates to his departure from Holland, or send me the sheets, wch. may be directed to me and inclosed under cover to The Lord Bishop of Clogher, etc. etc. etc. The Castle,

[1] Nichols, *Illust.* VIII, 673.

Dublin. I hope you will contrive to convey to me as directed the collection of Dr. Goldsmith's Misc. Essays, wch. you wished me to inspect, that your intended edition may not be retarded. This will oblige,

Gentlemen,

Your obedient humble servant,

Thos. Dromore.

Their prompt compliance is shown by the second letter referred to, written by Percy on July 15, 1798, from Dublin:

Gentlemen,

I shall order the copy of Goldsmith's Miscellanies to be returned you, which were only detained in hopes of getting an opportunity of sending them to me. To send a copy of them hither to me yourselves direct it for the Bishop of Dromore in care of Mr. John Archer of Dublin, at Messrs. Vernon and Hood, Poultry, Lond.

I received the desired sheet copied from the Life of Goldsmith, and am, gentlemen,

Your obedt. humble servant,

Thos. Dromore.

This late information regarding the end of Goldsmith's Leyden stay must have been the anecdotes communicated by Dr Ellis, concerning the tulip bulbs, and Goldsmith's setting out on his continental tour penniless, all of which were duly incorporated in the Memoir. If on any other occasion Percy applied for permission to change his manuscript and was denied, time has failed to bring the slightest hint of it to light. It may well be that by 1802 his recollection became confused, and, forgetting that he had given them their choice of copying out the part referred to, or sending him the original sheets, he persuaded himself that they had deliberately withheld the manuscript.

After the Memoir left Percy's hands in April, 1798, until some time in 1800, there is no evidence to show that Percy relinquished his function as editor. In the latter year, forgetting, or ignoring, the terms of their agreement, Percy again requested a money advance to Catherine Goldsmith, who was then in great distress. However we may approve the humane motive of his act and share his exasperation at the publishers' delay, there is no doubt that the act constituted a breach of the agreement between them, and the publishers availed themselves of it to rid themselves of such a devious, formal, and fussy collaborator. Percy himself stated this as the cause of their quarrel, in a letter to John Nichols of May 19, 1802.[1] It is clear that the introduction of Rose as the new editor was a result, not a cause, of the quarrel, as Forster imagined. The letter to Nichols referred to reads in part:

The press-work...does honor to your printing-office[2]... but the proprietors would have done well to have consulted me in the selection and arrangement, for they omitted one of the very best productions of Goldsmith, although it had been particularly pointed out in the account of his Life,—his *Introduction to Brooke's Natural History*—and have only given the *Preface* to that work, far inferior to the former. This is what

---

[1] Nichols, *Illust.* VI, 583.
[2] Nichols finally did the printing but had no connection with the publishing of the edition.

they got by quarreling with one for only supplicating a little assistance in advance to Goldsmith's poor niece, who was starving, for I would have given them every advice and direction gratis; but they carried their ill-humour so far as to refuse to let me see and make corrections in the MS. Life of Goldsmith, which had been compiled under my direction etc.

From this letter, it seems clear that there was no "formal and final withdrawing" of the Bishop's name from the scheme, which Forster talks of; but that he merely held himself aloof after the quarrel, in cold disapproval, waiting for apologies and advances from the publishers which did not come.

At the time of the letter to Nichols cited above, in which Percy goes on to say that he has "only just looked into Vols. II and IV," he had obviously not yet discovered the work of the "Interpolator" in volume I. Had he done so he would not have forborne mentioning it in the list of mistakes and omissions of which he complains. He was aware, by August, however, that his Memoir had been tampered with, and in reply to a letter[1] of inquiry from Robert Nares, written in April, asking whether the Life "really proceeds from your information, as is confidently asserted, and if not, how much credit is due to it on its own account," Percy wrote giving the required information. Nares wrote in return, on August 28, as follows:

Many thanks for your kind information on the subject of Goldsmith's life. If I take any advantage of what you mention

[1] Nichols, *Illust.* VII, 596.

in noticing the book, it shall be in such a way as cannot implicate you, or lead to any knowledge of its coming from you.[1]

What that "kind information" was which Percy sent can be inferred from the review of the edition which Nares wrote for the *British Critic* in September, 1802:

> It happens to be known to us, though by what channel we are not at liberty to say, that the materials have been collected from the most authentic sources, in a great measure from the relations of the poet himself, and digested and arranged under the eye of a Writer who to many other qualifications added an intimate knowledge of the person described. Who the medical friend was, who communicated a few of the anecdotes, we are not informed; but of the rest we can speak with confidence; and of that part we cannot but say that it bears strong marks of authenticity.

Percy and Malone seem to have remained in the dark as to the identity of the medical friend, as well as of the interpolator himself, since Malone, in writing to Percy as late as September 28, 1807, refers to him merely as "the Interpolator." It is well known now, however, both through Prior and Nichols, that the editor was Samuel Rose. The medical friend, whose anecdotes constituted the chief intrusions into the Memoir, Prior identified as Dr William Farr, a fellow student of Goldsmith's Edinburgh days; but Prior failed to identify the Farr anecdotes with the interpolations in the Memoir. The failure is the more surprising in view of the fact that Farr was Samuel Rose's father-in-law, a

---

[1] Nichols, *Illust.* VII, 598.

fact with which Prior was acquainted. Nothing could have been more in the natural order of things than for Rose to have incorporated the authentic memories of his own father-in-law concerning Goldsmith. In the following analysis of the Memoir's sources, the contributions of Rose, obtained from Farr, will be duly pointed out.

And so, finally, in the spring of 1802, after copyright troubles, disagreements, deaths, and all dissevering forces, not to mention Percy's morbidly sensitive temper, had worked against its completion, the Memoir appeared. For the subsequent difficulties in getting the 250 copies sold, the reader is referred to Nichols' *Literary Illustrations*, vol. VII, page 189, where they are described in a letter of Percy's to Robert Anderson. As to the aftermath of Percy's quarrel with Cadell and Davies, it is only necessary to explain here how it led to Percy's self-justifications, sent to Anderson, Malone, and others, which have helped to shed light on this history.

In 1804, when Percy had returned to Dromore, his literary correspondent, Robert Anderson, was trying to negotiate an agreement for the publication of a new edition of Percy's *Northern Antiquities*, and on May 6 he wrote to Percy[1] that Rees, the publisher, had refused to undertake it because of what Cadell and Davies had told him concerning the part Percy had taken in the edition of Goldsmith. He suggested at the same time that Percy should draw up a state-

---

[1] Anderson's correspondence with Percy referred to is found in Nichols, *Illust.* VII, 126–213.

ment of the matter to clear himself. Percy cannily refused to do so until he learned the exact nature of Cadell and Davies' accusations, and he spent the next eight months in sending intermittent hints to Anderson that a full statement would be acceptable. Finally, on June 3, 1805, Anderson, evidently embarrassed, sent him a hazy statement that Rees "peremptorily declined the undertaking...and said, from the account Mr. Davies had given him of your temper and conduct in the edition of Goldsmith, he would have no concern with you in any like undertaking whatever. He mentioned the bringing in of Boyd and other things of a troublesome kind." Percy finally put together his version of the matter in 1807, and sent it to Anderson, and to Malone, with the request that he show it to the members of the Club. This document, as I have already said, has, unfortunately, not been preserved. That the unpleasant business continued to be a subject of correspondence between him and Anderson is shown by a letter of the latter to Percy on May 15, 1811, in which he says, "In going over Goldsmith's Life, I will thank you to point out the particular passages which were thrust into your narrative." The Bishop died on September 30 of that year, and so it is doubtful if Anderson's request was ever answered. Indeed, so far as I know, the first attempt to "point out the particular passages" is recorded in the following section of this account.

Most of the facts of the Memoir can be traced to four sources—the written documents, already alluded to, in Percy's possession at the time of the Memoir's compilation; Percy's personal knowledge of Goldsmith; the stories contributed by Rose's father-in-law, Dr William Farr; and previously published anecdotes, chiefly borrowed from Glover's *Life of Dr. Oliver Goldsmith* (Swan, 1774), and Boswell's *Life of Johnson*. When the borrowing has been explicit, I have not pointed it out, nor have I attempted, with a few exceptions, to determine whether Percy or Rose was responsible for it. It seems certain, however, from the fact that Campbell mentions his intention[1] of including such parts of Boswell as "seem rightly stated," that he and Percy were responsible for some of the inclusions from that book, and it seems equally certain that the quotation of Johnson's unfavourable account, on page 20, of Goldsmith's knowledge and conversation, linked as it is with the remarks about Goldsmith's "grimacing and buffoonery," to which Malone took exception,[2] was inserted by Rose. It seems, therefore, safe to assume that the favourable quotations were included by Percy, and the unfavourable ones by Rose. Throughout the Memoir, Percy aimed at an ideal view of Goldsmith's character, and he admitted nothing that marred it.

[1] See the résumé of his letter of February 3, 1792, above.
[2] Prior, I, 445, letter of Percy to Malone, September 25, 1807.

No effort has been made to distinguish the individual contributions of Campbell and Boyd from Percy's, since, as has been pointed out, their workmanship was inextricably confused by the successive reworkings which the Memoir underwent while it was still in Percy's hands; furthermore, the facts, with a few exceptions which have been pointed out, were all Percy's. Matters of common information, such as the dates of Goldsmith's works, the reception of the poems and plays, Goldsmith's connection with the Royal Academy, have been attributed to Percy, on the assumption that such well-known facts must have been included in the Memoir before it left his hands.

The pagination references are to the sole edition of the Memoir, volume 1 of Goldsmith's *Miscellaneous Works*, London, 1801.

Page

1. Date of birth.	From a "member of Goldsmith's family," probably Maurice, who sent the information to Percy. See note to p. 116 of the Memoir, and Percy's MS. Memorandum, printed above.
1. Place of birth.	From Percy's Memorandum, *q.v.* The wording is borrowed.
2. Information about family.	From Percy's Memorandum, *q.v.* Also Dr Law. See p. 2 of the Memoir.
3–14. Facts of early life.	From the Hodson narrative.[1]
14, 16, 17. Facts from College records.	From Dr Wilson's letter to Malone.[2]

[1] The text of this narrative is to be published in the forthcoming edition of Goldsmith's Collected Letters.

[2] A copy of this letter is in Miss Meade's collection. Prior published it in part (1, 63–64, and 76–77), but omits, among other points, the speculation that he retired into the country.

Page

15. Tuition under Theaker Wilder.	From Dr Wilson's letter, the Hodson narrative, and Percy's Memorandum, *q.v.*
15. "Lounging about the college gate."	From a contemporary, probably Dr Wolfen. See p. 17 of the Memoir. Probably included by Percy.
16. Censure for taking part in a riot.	From Wilson's letter.
17. Speculation that he retired into the country.	From Wilson's letter.
17. Date of degree, Feb. 27, 1749, o.s.	From Wilson's letter. Doubt cast by Kearney. See above, p. 38.
17–19. Uncle Contarine's aid.	From the Hodson narrative and Percy's Memorandum, *q.v.*
19. Date of departure for Edinburgh, "end of 1752 or beginning of 1753."	A compromise by Percy between Mrs Hodson's statement of 1753 and the Memorandum's statement of 1751. Percy did not know Goldsmith's letter of September 26, 1753, which establishes the date as the autumn of 1752.
19. Anecdotes of his student life in Edinburgh.	Probably interpolated by Rose from Farr's information, although these are not specifically credited to the "medical friend."
19–20. Goldsmith's grimacing and buffoonery.	Interpolated by Rose from Farr's information. See Malone's letter to Percy, Prior, I, 445—"I never observed any of the grimaces and fooleries the interpolator talks of."
21. Studies and life in Edinburgh.	From Percy's Memorandum, *q.v.*
21. Dissipation.	Probably interpolated by Rose, from Farr's information.
21. Contemporary witness to poetical talents shown at Edinburgh.	From Glover's *Life*, London, 1774, also *Annual Register*, 1774, pt. 2, p. 30.

Page

22–26. Letter to Bob Bryanton.	In packet of letters sent to Percy by Maurice Goldsmith, and remaining in the Meade collection. The letter was a copy of the original, which was retained by the Bryanton family.
26. Debt contracted for a fellow-student.	From Glover's *Life*, and *Annual Register*, 1774, pt. 2, p. 30. Percy corrects "Sunderland" to "Newcastle," from the information in Goldsmith's letter to his Uncle Contarine from Leyden.
27–32. Letter to Uncle Contarine from Leyden.	Sent to Percy by Maurice Goldsmith on June 9, 1785,[1] and remaining in the Meade collection.
33–34. His gaming, the tulip anecdote, and his penniless state on setting out for France.	From Dr Ellis, a fellow-student of Goldsmith's at Leyden, and inserted by Percy in the summer of 1798, after the MS. of the Memoir had been turned over to the publishers. See the history of the Memoir above.
34. Entertainment at Irish convents.	From Percy's Memorandum, *q.v.*
34. Quotations from *Enquiry* and *Vicar* to illustrate his travels.	The *Vicar* quotation was first used by Glover, as if from Goldsmith's own mouth. The one from the *Enquiry* was first used by Malone, in the Dublin edition of the *Poems*, in 1777.
35. "Disputing his way through Europe."	Boswell first tells this story, *Life*, I, 411. Rose is probably responsible for its insertion here, since the quotation, "Thus...I fought my way," from Chap. xx of the *Vicar*, is inserted as if it

---

[1] Clarke, *Nineteenth Cent.* LXXV, 52. Maurice's accompanying letter has disappeared from the Meade collection since Clarke examined it.

Page

	were an autobiographical story of Goldsmith's from his own lips. Percy would have been more judicious.
35. Travels through Flanders, France, Germany, and Switzerland.	From Glover's *Life*, and *Annual Register*, pt. 2, pp. 29–30.
35. Comparison to Addison.	Suggested by Campbell. See letter of September 9, 1790, to Percy.
35–6. Doubts of tutor story, on grounds of resemblance to *Vicar*.	A refutation of Glover's account. "Intimate friends" suggests Percy as source.
36. Stay in Italy, six months in Padua, death of Uncle Contarine, return, date of arrival in England.	From Percy's Memorandum, *q.v.*
36. "If he ever took any medical degree it was probably in this school" (Padua).	From Percy. The Memorandum shows that he doubted Goldsmith's word about his M.B.'s being from Dublin, at "about 20," in 1750. Percy was present when Goldsmith took his *ad eundem* degree at Oxford, Feb. 26, 1769, when he said the degree was from Dublin.[1]
36. Note on *ad eundem* degree.	From Percy. See comment above.
37. Application for an ushership and letter to Dr Radcliff.	From Campbell, first published in his *Philosophical Survey of the South of Ireland* (p. 287), from Mrs Radcliff's information.
38. Goldsmith's remarks on the trials of the poor usher.	I cannot assign this.
38. Employment by chemist and assistance from Dr Sleigh.	First published in Malone's Dublin edition of 1777.[2] Cooke expands the story in 1793.[3] Percy probably inserted it in the Memoir.

---

[1] Clarke, *Nineteenth Cent.* LXXV, 829.
[2] *Poems and Plays of Oliver Goldsmith*, p. v.
[3] *European Magazine*, XXIV, 91.

Page

38. Practice of physic on the Bankside and removal to Temple. "Plenty of patients but no fees."

From Percy's Memorandum, *q.v.*

39–40. Account by friend of Goldsmith's tragedy, and his desire to decipher the "written mountains."

Interpolated by Rose, from information of Dr Farr.[1]

40–5. Letter to Dan Hodson.

In packet of letters sent to Percy by Maurice Goldsmith, and remaining in the Meade collection.

45. Engagement with Milner, East India appointment, etc.

From Percy's Memorandum, (*q.v.*), with the date of his medical appointment changed from 1757 to 1758, and the appointment itself described as "some medical appointment under the East India Company," in place of the Memorandum's "place of chief surgeon aboard an Indiaman."

46–59. Letters to Dan Hodson, Edward Mills, and Henry Goldsmith.

In packet of letters sent to Percy by Maurice Goldsmith, and remaining in the Meade collection.

60. Speculation that Goldsmith had given up his East India plan at the time of his letter to Henry.

From Percy, who met Goldsmith at Grainger's on February 21 of this year (1759).[2] From this point forward, Percy had an intimate personal knowledge of almost everything he inserts.

60. Engagement with Griffiths, break, and removal to Green Arbour Court.

From Percy's Memorandum, *q.v.* Percy changes the definite "£100" to "a handsome salary."

60–1. Incident of the chamber-pot of coals.

From Percy, sent to Campbell for inclusion in the Memoir. See Campbell's letter to Percy of June 30, 1790, above.

---

[1] Prior, I, 212.
[2] Gaussen, *Percy, Prelate and Poet*, p. 148.

Page

61. Removal to Wine-office Court.	From Percy's Memorandum and personal knowledge.[1]
61. Johnson's sale of the *Vicar* MS.	Obviously borrowed from Boswell's account. It offers nothing new, and does not sound like first-hand information.
61. The medical friend's opinion of the *Vicar*.	Interpolated by Rose, from information of Dr Farr.
62. Johnson's first visit to Goldsmith.	From Percy, sent to Campbell for inclusion in the Memoir. See Campbell's letter of June 30, 1790, above.
63. Lodgings at Canonbury in 1763.	From Percy. See the Memorandum.
63. Connection with Newbery, and publications of this period.	From Percy, sent to Campbell at his request. See Campbell's letter of June 30, 1790, above.
64. Hack-work of this period.	From Percy. The extracts from his diaries[2] state that he gave Goldsmith, on May 25, 1761, material for a "magazine of which he was then editor," i.e. the *Ladies' Magazine*.
65. Petition to Lord Bute.	From Percy. See the letter to Malone, of October 17, 1786, in the Adam collection, printed above.
66. Interview with the Earl of Northumberland's groom of the chambers.	From Percy, who, according to the text, discussed the incident with the Earl.
67–8. Hawkins' account of Goldsmith and Northumberland. Censure of Hawkins.	From Campbell. He expressed his intention of berating Hawkins in his letter to Percy of June 30, 1790, *q.v.*

---

[1] *Ibid.* p. 142.
[2] Gaussen, *Percy, Prelate and Poet*, p. 142.

Page

68–9. Further anecdotes of Goldsmith and the Duke and Duchess of Northumberland.

From Percy, who was the Duke's chaplain.

69. Changes of residence.

From Percy, who visited him in all these places. See the Memorandum. He omits his second residence in Garden Court, in 1767.

69–73. The Club.

From Percy. He kept a careful record of its activities, after his election on February 15, 1768, and entitled the extracts he made from them, "Extracts relating to Dr. Goldsmith and the Club to Goldsmith's death."[1]

74–6. *The Hermit* and its relation to Percy's *Friar of Orders Grey*.

From Percy.

77. Account of *The Good Natured Man, The Deserted Village*, histories, etc.

Common knowledge, probably inserted by Percy.

78–9. Memoranda of agreements with Davies.

From Percy, who had the original agreements, possibly from the younger Cadell, the publisher, whose father, Thomas Cadell, secured from Tom Davies his copyright to the English and Roman Histories. The agreements remain in the Meade collection.

79–82. Censure of Goldsmith's account of the Rev. George Walker.

From Percy and Campbell. It is based on a letter from Thomas Woolsey to Goldsmith, dated April 10, 1772, printed on pp. 80–81 of the Memoir, which must have formed part of the papers handed over to Percy by Goldsmith in 1773, although it does not remain in the Meade collection. The fact that Campbell was an ardent Irishman strengthens the supposition that he was responsible for this.

[1] Clarke, *Proc. Royal Soc. Med.* VII, pt. 2, p. 94.

Page

82–3. Goldsmith's Prefaces.

From Percy. In a letter to Nichols in 1802, quoted in the previous section, he berates the publishers for omitting the *Introduction* to Brookes' *Natural History*, "although it had been particularly pointed out in the Life."

83–4. *Life of Parnell*, and Johnson's tribute from the *Lives of the Poets*.

Probably from Percy and Campbell. Campbell wrote, on June 30, 1790, "Having *Parnell's Life*, I will return yours safe."

84. *The Beauties of English Poetry*.

Probably from Percy. The explanation of the accident by which the tale from Prior was included sounds sufficiently Bowdlerized to suggest Percy as the source.

85. Refutation of story about the payment for the *Deserted Village*.

I cannot assign this.

86. Election to Royal Academy.

Common knowledge, probably inserted by Percy.

86–9. Letter to Maurice Goldsmith.

In packet of letters sent to Percy by Maurice Goldsmith, and remaining in the Meade collection.

86–7. Note on Maurice Goldsmith.

From Percy. For his connection with Maurice, see the previous section of this article.

90–2. Letter to Sir Joshua Reynolds.

From Percy. It is still in the Meade collection, and was given to Percy by Boswell, who has added a marginal note, "Original letter of Dr. Goldsmith to Sir Joshua Reynolds who gave it to me."

92. Invitation from Bennet Langton.

From Percy. The original letter from Langton is in the Percy collection, and was evidently in the packet of papers given to Percy by Goldsmith in 1773.

Page

92–4. Goldsmith's reply.

From Percy. It was "published by Langton's permission," and was evidently given to Percy by Langton. It is still in the Meade collection.

95–8. Letters from Oglethorpe and Paine.

Percy's selection from the papers given him by Goldsmith in 1773. They remain in the Meade collection.

99. The Pilkington story.

Appeared first in the *London Chronicle* for September 6–9, 1777, and again in the *European Magazine* for October, 1793, in Cooke's anecdotes of Goldsmith. This is probably one of the "basket of absurdities" alluded to by Campbell, in his letter of June 30, 1790, *q.v.* It is obviously not based on new material.

99–100. Anecdotes of the Chevalier de Champigny and Griffin.

Based on letters given to Percy by Goldsmith in 1773, printed by Miss Gaussen[1] from the Meade collection.

100–10. *She Stoops to Conquer* and the affray with Evans.

From the materials given to Percy by Goldsmith in 1773, remaining in the Meade collection. Percy was the "amanuensis" referred to on p. 105.[2]

110. Anecdote of Johnson and Lord Eliot.

Interpolated by Rose, from information of Dr Farr.

110–11, 113. *History of Animated Nature*, period of composition, style, use of Buffon, etc.

From Percy. Sixteen folio pages of Goldsmith's original MS. of *Animated Nature* remain in the Meade collection.

111. Gaming and debts to the booksellers.

First made public in Davies' *Life of Garrick*, 1780.[3] The facts were

---

[1] *Percy, Prelate and Poet*, p. 147. These letters no longer remain in the Meade collection.

[2] Clarke, *Trans. Bib. Soc.* XV, p. 30.   [3] II, 156–7.

Page

	probably widely known among his friends. Percy may be responsible for their inclusion.
112. *The Haunch of Venison* and *Retaliation*.	Common knowledge; no new information added. Probably from Percy.
112. The *Dictionary of Arts and Sciences* and the Prospectus.	From Percy. Percy's attempt to trace the MS., through the agency of Malone and Boswell, is chronicled in the previous section of this account.
113. The facility of Goldsmith's prose style—"whole quires of...*Animated Nature*, etc." unaltered.	From Percy. See the comment on *Animated Nature* above.
113. Goldsmith's chronic illness.	From Percy. The extracts from the pocket-books show that Percy had visited him on September 21, 1772, and "found him ill."[1]
113–15. Last illness and death.	From Percy. The extracts again show that Percy visited him on March 28, near the beginning of his illness, and again on April 3, the day before his death. After his death, he saw the coffin on April 9, but apparently did not attend the funeral.[2]
116. Epitaph.	From the monument in Westminster Abbey.
116. Note correcting the year of his birth.	The note says this came from a "member of the family," probably Maurice. It is clear, however, that the date of the epitaph coincides with Goldsmith's own statement in Percy's Memorandum (*q.v.*), in which he says he was born "in 1731 (or 1730).

[1] Gaussen, *Percy, Prelate and Poet*, p. 168.
[2] *Ibid.* pp. 168–9.